BLOOP ANIMATION'S

Storyboard Notebook

PROPERTY OF

....
Name

....
Contact information (Please return if found!)

Copyright © 2022 by Bloop Animation Studios LLC

All Rights Reserved. No part of this book may be reproduced or used in any form or by any means, electronic or mechanical, including photocopying, recording, or by any information storage and retrieval system, without permission in writing from the publisher, unless faithfully conforming to fair use guidelines.

Contents

Title   Page

Title	Page

Title	Page

How to Use This Book

THIS BOOK WILL PRESENT YOU with three unique storyboard templates. Each is designed for a different part of the process, or different working styles. Explore all three to find what works best for you, or switch from one to the next as your project progresses.

THUMBNAIL (opposite): Designed for quick sketches, a great way to get your initial ideas down on paper. We included many panels on each page to make it easier to get a feeling for the rhythm of your scene as you work. This template does not include any lines for dialogue or action.

FLEXIBLE (page 8): Designed to be clean and simple, but includes text lines for action and dialogue. This template works for most projects as it is quick to get started with, but allows for adding direction notes as needed.

PROFESSIONAL (page 9): Designed with professional production needs in mind, this template allows for the most amount of details, following standard production practices. Each panel includes boxes for scene/shot/panel numbers, as well as dedicated action and dialogue lines.

Title: **UNDEFEATED** Scene: **4**

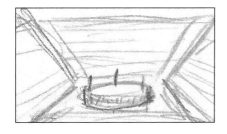

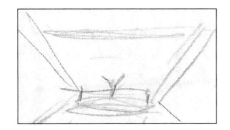

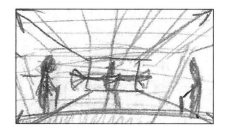
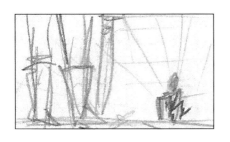
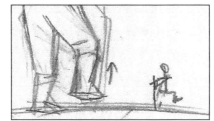

Title: **TASTEFUL - ANIMATED SHORT** Scene **3** 8

FISHY OFFERS PIGGY THE PORK TACOS

PIGGY SLAPS THE TACO AWAY

PIGGY SLAMS THE TACOS ON GROUND

PIGGY STARES AT FISHY FOR A MOMENT BEFORE-

-WALKING AWAY ANGRY

Title: TLZ - 2.28
9

Scene 1 | Shot 17 | Panel 1

Dialogue: PADGETT: "CHECKING OUT A REPORT OF AN UNIDENTIFIED FLYING OBJECT. SUPPOSED TO HAVE LANDED IN THE AREA OF HOOK'S LANDING."

Action:

Scene 1 | Shot 18 | Panel 1

Dialogue: PADGETT: "CAME DOWN IN THE ICE AT TRACEY'S POND AND WE CAN'T SEE IT NOW."

Action:

Scene 1 | Shot 19 | Panel 1

Dialogue:

Action: PERRY TRUDGES BACK TOWARD THE CAR. BACKTRACKING OVER THE PATH HE TROD

Title .... Scene 10

TEMPLATE #1

Thumbnails

Title .... Scene 12

Title .... Scene 15

Title .... Scene 16

Title .... Scene 17

Title .... Scene 18

Title .... Scene 19

Title .... Scene 20

Title .... Scene 21

Title .... Scene 22

Title .... Scene 23

Title .... Scene 24

Title .... Scene 25

Title .... Scene 26

Title .... Scene 27

Title .... Scene 28

Title .... Scene 29

Title .... Scene 30

Title .... Scene 31

Title .... Scene 32

Title .... Scene 33

Title .... Scene 34

Title .... Scene 35

Title .... Scene 36

Title .... Scene 37

Title .... Scene 38

Title .... Scene 39

Title .... Scene 40

Title .... Scene 41

Title .... Scene 42

Title .... Scene 43

Title .... Scene 44

Title .... Scene 45

Title .... Scene 46

Title .... Scene 47

Title .... Scene 48

Title .... Scene 49

Title .... Scene 50

Title .... Scene 51

Title .... Scene 52

Title .... Scene 53

Title .... Scene 54

Title .... Scene 55

Title .... Scene 56

Title .... Scene 57

Title .... Scene 58

Title .... Scene 59

Title .... Scene 60

Title .... Scene 61

Title .... Scene 62

Title .... Scene 63

Title .... Scene 64

Title .... Scene 65

Title .... Scene 66

Title .... Scene 67

Title .... Scene 68

Title .... Scene 69

Title .... Scene 70

Title .... Scene 71

Title .... Scene 72

TEMPLATE #2

Flexible

Title .... Scene 74

Title .... Scene 75

Title .... Scene 76

Title .... Scene 77

Title ....

Title .... Scene 78

Title .... Scene 79

Title .... Scene 80

Title .... Scene 81

Title .... Scene 82

Title .... Scene 83

Title .... Scene 84

Title .... Scene 85

Title .... Scene 86

Title .... Scene 87

Title .... Scene 88

Title .... Scene 89

Title .... Scene 90

Title .... Scene 91

Title .... Scene 92

Title .... Scene 93

Title .... Scene 94

Title .... Scene 95

Title .... Scene 96

Title .... Scene 97

Title .... Scene 98

Title .... Scene 99

Title .... Scene 100

Title .... Scene 101

Title .... Scene 102

Title .... Scene 103

Title .... Scene 104

Title .... Scene 105

Title .... Scene 106

Title .... Scene ....

Title .... Scene 108

Title .... Scene 109

Title .... Scene 110

Title .... Scene 111

Title .... Scene 112

Title .... Scene 113

Title .... Scene 114

Title .... Scene 115

Title .... Scene 116

Title .... Scene 117

Title .... Scene 118

Title .... Scene 119

Title .... Scene 120

Title Scene 121

Title .... Scene 122

Title .... Scene 123

Title .... Scene 124

Title .... Scene 125

Title .... Scene 126

Title .... Scene 127

Title .... Scene 128

Title .... Scene 129

Title .... Scene 130

Title .... Scene 131

Title .... Scene 132

Title .... Scene 133

Title .... Scene 134

Title .... Scene 135

Title

| Scene | Shot | Panel |

Dialogue

Action

| Scene | Shot | Panel |

Dialogue

Action

Dialogue

| Scene | Shot | Panel |

Dialogue

Action

TEMPLATE #3

Professional

Title

| Scene | Shot | Panel |

Dialogue

Action

| Scene | Shot | Panel |

Dialogue

Action

| Scene | Shot | Panel |

Dialogue

Action

Title

Scene	Shot	Panel

Dialogue

Action

Scene	Shot	Panel

Dialogue

Action

Scene	Shot	Panel

Dialogue

Action

Title ....

Scene	Shot	Panel

Dialogue

Action

Scene	Shot	Panel

Dialogue

Action

Scene	Shot	Panel

Dialogue

Action

Title

| Scene | Shot | Panel |

Dialogue

Action

| Scene | Shot | Panel |

Dialogue

Action

| Scene | Shot | Panel |

Dialogue

Action

Title ....

Scene	Shot	Panel

Dialogue
....
....
....
....
....

Action
....
....
....
....

Scene	Shot	Panel

Dialogue
....
....
....
....
....

Action
....
....
....
....

Scene	Shot	Panel

Dialogue
....
....
....
....
....

Action
....
....
....
....

Title

| Scene | Shot | Panel |

Dialogue

Action

| Scene | Shot | Panel |

Dialogue

Action

| Scene | Shot | Panel |

Dialogue

Action

Title

Scene	Shot	Panel

Dialogue

Action

Scene	Shot	Panel

Dialogue

Action

Scene	Shot	Panel

Dialogue

Action

Title ....

Scene	Shot	Panel

Dialogue

Action

Scene	Shot	Panel

Dialogue

Action

Scene	Shot	Panel

Dialogue

Action

Title ....

Scene	Shot	Panel

Dialogue

Action

Scene	Shot	Panel

Dialogue

Action

Scene	Shot	Panel

Dialogue

Action

Title 147

Scene	Shot	Panel

Dialogue

Action

Scene	Shot	Panel

Dialogue

Action

Scene	Shot	Panel

Dialogue

Action

Title ....

Scene	Shot	Panel

Dialogue

Action

Scene	Shot	Panel

Dialogue

Action

Scene	Shot	Panel

Dialogue

Action

Title 149

| Scene | Shot | Panel |

Dialogue

Action

| Scene | Shot | Panel |

Dialogue

Action

| Scene | Shot | Panel |

Dialogue

Action

Title

Scene	Shot	Panel

Dialogue

Action

Scene	Shot	Panel

Dialogue

Action

Scene	Shot	Panel

Dialogue

Action

Title 151

| Scene | Shot | Panel |

Dialogue

Action

| Scene | Shot | Panel |

Dialogue

Action

| Scene | Shot | Panel |

Dialogue

Action

Title

| Scene | Shot | Panel |

Dialogue

Action

| Scene | Shot | Panel |

Dialogue

Action

| Scene | Shot | Panel |

Dialogue

Action

Title

Scene	Shot	Panel

Dialogue

Action

Scene	Shot	Panel

Dialogue

Action

Scene	Shot	Panel

Dialogue

Action

Title 154

Scene	Shot	Panel

Dialogue

Action

Scene	Shot	Panel

Dialogue

Action

Scene	Shot	Panel

Dialogue

Action

Title

| Scene | Shot | Panel |

Dialogue

Action

| Scene | Shot | Panel |

Dialogue

Action

| Scene | Shot | Panel |

Dialogue

Action

Title

Scene	Shot	Panel

Dialogue

Action

Scene	Shot	Panel

Dialogue

Action

Scene	Shot	Panel

Dialogue

Action

Title

| Scene | Shot | Panel |

Dialogue

Action

| Scene | Shot | Panel |

Dialogue

Action

| Scene | Shot | Panel |

Dialogue

Action

Title

Scene	Shot	Panel

Dialogue

Action

Scene	Shot	Panel

Dialogue

Action

Scene	Shot	Panel

Dialogue

Action

Title

| Scene | Shot | Panel |

Dialogue

Action

| Scene | Shot | Panel |

Dialogue

Action

| Scene | Shot | Panel |

Dialogue

Action

Title ....

Scene	Shot	Panel	Dialogue
			Action

Scene	Shot	Panel	Dialogue
			Action

Scene	Shot	Panel	Dialogue
			Action

Title

| Scene | Shot | Panel |

Dialogue

Action

| Scene | Shot | Panel |

Dialogue

Action

| Scene | Shot | Panel |

Dialogue

Action

Title 162

| Scene | Shot | Panel |

Dialogue

Action

| Scene | Shot | Panel |

Dialogue

Action

| Scene | Shot | Panel |

Dialogue

Action

Title

| Scene | Shot | Panel |

Dialogue

Action

| Scene | Shot | Panel |

Dialogue

Action

| Scene | Shot | Panel |

Dialogue

Action

Title

| Scene | Shot | Panel |

Dialogue

Action

| Scene | Shot | Panel |

Dialogue

Action

| Scene | Shot | Panel |

Dialogue

Action

Title

| Scene | Shot | Panel |

Dialogue

Action

| Scene | Shot | Panel |

Dialogue

Action

| Scene | Shot | Panel |

Dialogue

Action

Title

Scene	Shot	Panel

Dialogue

Action

Scene	Shot	Panel

Dialogue

Action

Scene	Shot	Panel

Dialogue

Action

Title

| Scene | Shot | Panel |

Dialogue

Action

| Scene | Shot | Panel |

Dialogue

Action

| Scene | Shot | Panel |

Dialogue

Action

Title

Scene	Shot	Panel

Dialogue

Action

Scene	Shot	Panel

Dialogue

Action

Scene	Shot	Panel

Dialogue

Action

Title

| Scene | Shot | Panel |

Dialogue

Action

| Scene | Shot | Panel |

Dialogue

Action

| Scene | Shot | Panel |

Dialogue

Action

Title

Scene	Shot	Panel

Dialogue

Action

Scene	Shot	Panel

Dialogue

Action

Scene	Shot	Panel

Dialogue

Action

Title

Scene	Shot	Panel

Dialogue

Action

Scene	Shot	Panel

Dialogue

Action

Scene	Shot	Panel

Dialogue

Action

Title

Scene	Shot	Panel

Dialogue

Action

Scene	Shot	Panel

Dialogue

Action

Scene	Shot	Panel

Dialogue

Action

Title

| Scene | Shot | Panel |

Dialogue

Action

| Scene | Shot | Panel |

Dialogue

Action

| Scene | Shot | Panel |

Dialogue

Action

Title ....

Scene	Shot	Panel

Dialogue
....
....
....
....
....

Action
....
....
....
....

Scene	Shot	Panel

Dialogue
....
....
....
....
....

Action
....
....
....
....

Scene	Shot	Panel

Dialogue
....
....
....
....
....

Action
....
....
....
....

Title

| Scene | Shot | Panel |

Dialogue

Action

| Scene | Shot | Panel |

Dialogue

Action

| Scene | Shot | Panel |

Dialogue

Action

Title

| Scene | Shot | Panel |

Dialogue

Action

| Scene | Shot | Panel |

Dialogue

Action

| Scene | Shot | Panel |

Dialogue

Action

Title

Scene	Shot	Panel

Dialogue

Action

Scene	Shot	Panel

Dialogue

Action

Scene	Shot	Panel

Dialogue

Action

Title ....

Scene	Shot	Panel

Dialogue
....
....
....
....

Action
....
....
....
....

Scene	Shot	Panel

Dialogue
....
....
....
....

Action
....
....
....
....

Scene	Shot	Panel

Dialogue
....
....
....
....

Action
....
....
....
....

Title

Scene	Shot	Panel

Dialogue

Action

Scene	Shot	Panel

Dialogue

Action

Scene	Shot	Panel

Dialogue

Action

Title

| Scene | Shot | Panel |

Dialogue

Action

| Scene | Shot | Panel |

Dialogue

Action

| Scene | Shot | Panel |

Dialogue

Action

Title

| Scene | Shot | Panel |

Dialogue

Action

| Scene | Shot | Panel |

Dialogue

Action

| Scene | Shot | Panel |

Dialogue

Action

Title

Scene	Shot	Panel

Dialogue

Action

Scene	Shot	Panel

Dialogue

Action

Scene	Shot	Panel

Dialogue

Action

Title

| Scene | Shot | Panel |

Dialogue

Action

| Scene | Shot | Panel |

Dialogue

Action

| Scene | Shot | Panel |

Dialogue

Action

Title

Scene	Shot	Panel

Dialogue

Action

Scene	Shot	Panel

Dialogue

Action

Scene	Shot	Panel

Dialogue

Action

Title

Scene	Shot	Panel

Dialogue

Action

Scene	Shot	Panel

Dialogue

Action

Scene	Shot	Panel

Dialogue

Action

Title

186

Scene	Shot	Panel

Dialogue

Action

Scene	Shot	Panel

Dialogue

Action

Scene	Shot	Panel

Dialogue

Action

Title

| Scene | Shot | Panel |

Dialogue

Action

| Scene | Shot | Panel |

Dialogue

Action

| Scene | Shot | Panel |

Dialogue

Action

About Bloop Animation Studios

BLOOP ANIMATION STUDIOS is a leading animation training platform used by thousands of students, featuring hundreds of video lessons, articles, courses, and guidebooks about animation filmmaking.

www.bloopanimation.com

·

facebook.com/bloopanimation

·

youtube.com/bloopanimation

Made in the USA
Middletown, DE
02 October 2024